# Prayers
## at
# Eastertime

by Pamela Kennedy
Illustrated by Stephanie McFetridge Britt

D1534367

**ideals children's books**
Nashville, Tennessee

ISBN 0-8249-5366-5 (case)
ISBN 0-8249-5367-3 (paper)

Published by Ideals Children's Books
An imprint of Ideals Publications
A division of Guideposts
535 Metroplex Drive, Suite 250
Nashville, Tennessee 37211
www.idealspublications.com

Copyright © 1989 by Ideals Publications, a division of Guideposts

All rights reserved. No part of this publication may be reproduced or
transmitted in any form or by any means, electronic or mechanical,
including photocopy, recording, or any information storage and retrieval
system, without permission in writing from the publisher.

Printed and bound in Mexico by RR Donnelley & Sons.

Library of Congress CIP Data on file.

All Scriptures quoted are from the Holy Bible New International
Version. Copyright © 1973, 1978, 1984 by the International Bible
Society. Used by permission of Zondervan Bible Publishers.

10  8  6  4  2  1  3  5  7  9

pring is the time
for flying kites
and jumping rope,
for playing baseball
and for shooting marbles.

Did you play games when
you were little, Jesus?
If you were here,
I'd let you share my toys.

*Jesus said, "Let the little children come to me."*
Matthew 19:14

hank you for
the sounds
of spring, dear God—
the bubbling streams
and chirping birds,
the chattering chipmunks
and croaking frogs.

You make everything
sound so glad!

*See! The winter is past; the rains are*
*over and gone. Flowers appear on the*
*earth; the season of singing has come.*
Song of Solomon 2:11–12

 planted some seeds in my garden today, God. I covered them with dirt and I watered them with my sprinkling can.

But that's all I can do. Please send the rain and let the sun shine so my seeds will grow.

*I planted the seed . . . but God made it grow.*
1 Corinthians 3:6

esus, thank you
for the rain.
It makes rivers for my boats
and puddles for my boots
and squishy mud for pies.

I like to hear the drippy,
droppy rain song in the night.

*I will send you rain in its season.*
Leviticus 26:4

 was having so
much fun today,
Jesus, that I forgot to come
when Mama called.

And I wore my muddy boots
into the house. I think
I need to say, "I'm sorry
and I'll do better."

*The Lord is Lord of all and richly blesses*
*all who call on him.*
Romans 10:12

ometimes it's hard to wait for the rain to stop, for the seeds to grow, and for summer to finally come.

Do you ever get tired of waiting, Jesus? Maybe if we wait together, it won't seem so long.

*Be still before the Lord and wait patiently for him.*
Psalm 37:7

ear Jesus,
I feel sick today.
My head hurts and
my nose is stuffy.

Mama says it's a cold,
but I feel hot. Please help
me feel better, so I can
go out and play.

*O Lord, my God, I called to you*
*for help and you healed me.*
Psalm 30:2

esus, guess what
I found today?
They're gray and soft,
just like kittens, but
they grow on a stick.

Daddy says they're pussywillows,
and that means that spring
is here. Thank you for filling
the world with pretty things!

*The earth is the Lord's and everything in it.*
Psalm 24:1

ometimes I'm scared when there's a storm. The wind blows so hard that the trees creak. The lightning flashes and the thunder booms so loudly that my window rattles.

Then I remember that you are stronger than the storm, God, and it helps me not to be afraid.

*I will fear no evil for you are with me.*
Psalm 23:4

O n Easter Day
we go to church.
I love to smell the flowers
and hear the songs.

But the best part is to know
that you are still alive, Jesus,
and to remember that you
love even me.

*We love because he first loved us.*
1 John 4:19